thgow palooza readers

EMERGING 2 READER

Splishy, Splashy Mammals

By Susan Blackaby

School Specialty Publishing

Library of Congress Cataloging-in-Publication Data is on file with the publisher.

Send all inquiries to:
School Specialty Publishing
8720 Orion Place
Columbus, OH 43240-2111

ISBN 0-7696-4252-7

1 2 3 4 5 6 7 8 9 10 PHXBK 10 09 08 07 06

Hi, I'm a manatee.
Join me in learning about
mammals that live in and near the water.
I live in the water, but I am not a fish.
I am a mammal just like you!
Mammals are warm-blooded animals.
Most have hair and feed milk to their young.
Turn the page to learn more about mammals
that live in water homes.

Table of Contents

Manatee

Manatees live in water near **shores**.
The water is warm there
and not very deep.
Manatees eat plants and move slowly.
Sometimes, they are called "sea cows."

Blue Whale

The blue whale is the largest animal on the earth.
It is as big as 30 elephants.
Blue whales must live where the water is deep.
They live in oceans all over the world.

Orca

Orcas are known for their black
and white coloring.
These whales spend all of their lives
in the ocean.
Orcas swim fast and dive deep.
They have long **flippers**.
They also have strong **flukes**, or tails.

Humpback Whale

Humpback whales also live where
the ocean is deep.
They leap out of the sea
and crash down again.
This is called **breaching**.
Humpback whales have a **fin**
on their backs.
The fin looks like a hump.

Dolphin

Dolphins talk to each other
with squeaks and chirps.
They live in small **pods**, or groups.
Dolphins swim together in the deep sea.
They hunt for fish and squid.

Elephant Seal

Elephant seals spend most of their lives
in cold ocean water.
They can stay underwater
for a long time.
Some elephant seals have big noses.
Their noses look like an elephant's trunk.

Harbor Seal

Harbor seals cannot walk.
They swim in the water most of the time.
They flop onto the beach.
There, they sit in the sun.

Sea Lion

Sea lions live in and out of the ocean.
They swim and splash in the water.
They paddle with their front flippers.
They steer with their back flippers.
They also use their back flippers
to walk on land.

Sea Otter

Sea otters spend their lives in cold
ocean water.
Thick, oily fur keeps them warm.
Otters dive for **shellfish**.
They float on their backs to eat.
They use their chests like tables.
They crack open shells with rocks.

River Otter

River otters are like sea otters.
But they live in **freshwater**.
River otters eat fish and snakes.
They eat frogs and insects, too.
Webbed feet help river otters swim.

Beaver

Beavers spend a lot of time
in the water.
They live in streams, rivers, and lakes.
Beavers have short legs
and chunky bodies.
They have tails that look like
big paddles.
Beavers make **dams** out of
tree branches.

Muskrat

Muskrats live in **marshes**, streams, lakes, and ponds.
They eat lots of plants.
They also eat turtles and fish.
Muskrats make **dens** in the banks of streams.

Raccoon

Raccoons live all over
the United States.
But they like to be near water, such as
lakes and streams.
Raccoons are good swimmers.
They eat crabs, fish, and frogs.
They eat fruit, nuts, and seeds, too.

Vocabulary

breaching–breaking through. *Breaching whales leap out of the water and crash back down.*

dam–a nest made of trees built by beavers. *There is a beaver dam in the river behind my house.*

den–a living space made and used by animals as a shelter. *We saw a muskrat crawl into its den.*

fin–a thin, flat body part of an aquatic animal used for swimming or balance. *The shark's fin stuck out of the water.*

flipper–a broad, flat limb used for swimming. *A seal has strong flippers.*

fluke–one of the two rounded halves of a whale's tail. *The whale slapped its flukes on the water.*

freshwater–water that is not salty or part of the sea. *Beavers live in freshwater.*

marsh–a soft, wet lowland often covered with water. *A muskrat eats plants in the shallow water of the marsh.*

pod–a group of marine mammals. *A pod of dolphins swam by the boat.*

shellfish–water animals with a shell. *Oysters, clams, and crabs are shellfish.*

shore–the land along the edges of oceans, lakes, and rivers. *Manatees swim in water close to shores.*

Think About It!

1. Why do you think manatees are called "sea cows"? How are they similar to cows?
2. Which animals in the book live in water all of the time? Which animals live in water some of the time?
3. What is the largest animal on the earth? Where does this animal live?
4. How might dolphin pods be like human families?
5. How is a river otter different from a sea otter?

The Story and You!

1. What is your favorite mammal from the book?
2. Have you ever seen these mammals before? Where?
3. If you were an animal, would you rather live in the water or on land? Why?
4. Have you heard the saying "busy as a beaver"? What do you think this saying means?